CW01082683

FRET NOT

poems by

MICHAEL SHINDLER

Finishing Line Press
Georgetown, Kentucky

FRET NOT

ACKNOWLEDGMENTS

These poems have appeared in various publications (though in some instances in slightly different forms):

"A Pinewood" appeared in *Ekstasis;*
"Pan is in the Wood" and "On the Bridge" in *Apocalypse Confidential;*
"Invocation" (originally under the title, "Sing Now") in *The Imaginative Conservative;*
"Epilogue" (originally under the title, "When I Grow"), "We Walk," "Go and Gather" (originally under the title "Go and Gather Me Flowers"), "A White Stag," "We Had Heard Them," "The Trees," "Away," "A Great Ox," "A Purple," "A Satyr," "A Fruit Tree," "A Lone Thief," "Lovers Dancing," "A Willow Branch," "A Bird of Prey," "A Hero Long-Returned," "We are Almost," "A Whisper," "Crowds that Meet," "A Seamstress," and "My Daughter" in *The New English Review.*

I thank the editors of these publications, particularly Kendra Mallock, Alyssa Barnes, Mike Bonikowsky, and Tom Will.

Additionally, I thank my friend and fellow poet (as well as career diplomat, philosopher, educator, jazz connoisseur, and so on) Dennis Skocz, for his comments and conversation regarding these poems and poetry generally.

Publisher: Leah Huete de Maines
Editor: Christen Kincaid
Cover Art: Giorgione, *The Tempest*
Author Photo: Madeline Yarbrough
Cover Design: Elizabeth Maines McCleavy

Order online: www.finishinglinepress.com
also available on amazon.com

Author inquiries and mail orders:
Finishing Line Press
PO Box 1626
Georgetown, Kentucky 40324
USA

Contents

INVOCATION

Sing now child in the valley-glade.
Fret not over the blind judgment
Of hyacinths
Or high pines yielding welcome shade.

Your hair's neither darkened nor grayed
Nor lost in the throes of lament;
But your will is by beauty bent
And though that too in time will fade,
Fret not.

WE WALK

We walk on the forest floor, you and I,
Beyond the bounds of lined fields and firelight,
Seeing only shapes of the wild and sky
So that all the world seems one woodland-sight,
And we feel these shapes touching us gently:
The stroke of a vine, the tap of a tree;
We're forgetting each plant's proper naming,
Classifications we've learnt from reading;
We stop recalling the links and logic,
Accounts of the world's internal working,
And I wonder—do you hear strange music?

Our thoughts become theaters where branches vie
With one another and warm lengths of light
Pass through thickets and potent shadows lie
Alongside flowers, without fret or fight,
And birds trill high above with guiltless glee
Within the whisper of the canopy;
Amid this mass of oaks, we are walking
As they march up the hillside, enduring
Through every storm's jest and every drought's trick
With their trunks swelling and branches soaring.

Our father was here, where lost songbirds fly,
In the past, right here, in this selfsame site:
Right here would he laugh, right here would he cry,
Laboring by day and dreaming by night;
This was his home; this was where he was free:
One day our father climbed up high to see
The glory of heaven, the sun shining,
And when he climbed down, it was by hugging
The trees that he learnt to stand like this stick,
His feet on earth, his eyes upward looking.

As we walk, we see things growing nearby
And shrinking and stretching without respite;
We watch the shifting of the clouds up high
Unworried with how they'll next shift in flight,
But with a regard that extends broadly
To all these shapes that in dusk's lambency
Seem to shift like one immense thing moving:
A petal in play with wind while falling,
A spider weaving where the grass grows thick,
A bit of lightning in clouds gathering.

In both our bodies air is flowing by
Nutrients flowing down then up our height,
Surging with the air, with silence and sigh,
The dance of the forest's diurnal rite;
Opposed things coming and going promptly:
You and I walking through the greenery;
Our bodies, our minds, our thoughts, are taking
Us deeper into the shapes of the thing;
That which makes the journey true and tragic
Is bringing us here, where all is growing,
And I wonder—do you hear strange music?

A SATYR

A satyr singing in the mist,
A fig tree behind him,
A bangle on his wrist,
And the world at his whim:

'The clouds race, the birds chase,
And night comes like a thief;
Songs are sweet, men must eat,
But glory tastes of grief.'

A LONE THIEF

A lone thief in the company of dimming oaks
Crept with the whistling wind,
His wine-red lips grinning
At a dozen half-remembered jokes.
But he came to a place where the oak-canopy thinned
And saw there a bright angel spinning,
His sword shearing constellations.

GO AND GATHER

Go and gather me flowers from afar
When the nights are warm,
Beneath a blue-black star;
Listen and follow, listen and follow
—the dying sound, which crickets hallow,
A song of the wind sung in the storm:

'The new dawn rides near; the low-clouds are red.
There has been a death, there has been a birth,
Though the flowers lie dead upon the earth,
White flowers stand in the land of the dead.'

A WHITE STAG

'A white stag, a white stag,
How many hands is he high?
Are his antlers silver?
And is the sea in his eye?'

A strange clang, a strange clang
From the antlers and the sword.
Together we had come:
One a king and one a lord.

'Where goes he, where goes he?
He who was but in my hand;
There he was; there he fell
Like a shadow falls on land.'

A HERO LONG-RETURNED

A hero long-returned from
The vicissitudes of rude adventuring
With a withered coronal of violets
On his gilded brow
Strums
A song of gilded suffering
And permits
Himself to avow:

'That every hour is a type of peace,
Which the heavy mind can dwell in;
That every cut-flower is on lease,
Which perhaps Paris knew of Helen.'

A GREAT OX

A great ox like a hill in a barren field
Standing black against the dawn
With body once broken, now healed,
With silver-mended horns and brawn:

He pushed past the sun
And the mountains, unplowed immensities,
And with his silver won
A briar-crown of vanities.

WE HAD HEARD THEM

We had heard them in the clouds overhead
Above the sun that had begun to fall
And the field where flicker the fallen dead:
Above you and me, but not above all.
And what a strange sound they make as they fly
As we go with the whirl of the world by.
But it is a good sound, that sound that went
In the moments that marked our day's descent:
It came down in the silence of the hour
Then left that hour and the silence content.

You and I had went where that sound had led,
Racing one another at the high wall
Till our footfalls fell in—in that race wed
Like two faraway stars spied at nightfall:
At the first a lonesome light to the eye,
But which darkling hours split with a sigh.
And what all the sound and the starlight meant,
And what their absences now represent
Shades a lone eye as branches a bower
Where they had been but for an hour pent.

Where did those stars go? Is that field their bed?
Did they both come at one another's call,
As if tied and towed by a common thread?
Do not tell me until I can recall.
The way of the field and way of the sky
Are from each to each a sort of reply,
Which must be gotten and which must be sent
Without regret and yet without relent
By us two in that tall ashen tower
Standing midway within the world's extent.

And in that tower, what we both had said
Of what had been and of what would befall,
Of a faith and folly, of joy and dread,
It was true somehow—was good overall,
But the hour had passed, the sun rose high,
It had come time at last to say goodbye:
So you and I had went, with your head bent;
The sun in glory, the moon discontent;
It is what it is: out of our power.
But what it was—it lingers like a scent.

But where am I? Am I where you had fled?
The field is gone, the tower not so tall.
Was that sound a song? Are these clouds a bed?
The stars seem too large and the world too small.

THE TREES

The trees—they wake and turn
As the sun strikes the hill.
The winds upward churn
And she stands still.

The sun strikes above.
The trees grasp at its fire.
The winds stoke their lust to love.
Their cry slips into choir.

They free their fire and fade.
The winds elsewhere stray.
The sun is gone now from the glade
And she steps away.

AWAY

'Away—away to Apollo's bay,'
Sings the strife-worn choir.
'Away—away there we'll stray
Singing mad to Apollo's lyre.

'Flower petals are fine indeed,
But finer are the fingers of death;
From fear of fate are we freed
And the flowers fall in our breath.

'Away—we've gone to Apollo's bay
And the music is a flower-fire;
Away—we've seen the petals stray
And all that's left is Apollo's ire.'

LOVERS DANCING

Lovers dancing in the shadow of a cliffside,
Arms rising and falling,
From each to each calling,
Would-be husband to would-be bride:

'Listen—the suns stand.
The moons bow.'

And their dance, as they dance, is a deep breath.

'Listen—take my hand.
Make your vow.'

And so each called to each to death.

A PINEWOOD

A pinewood sways breathless
In heaving breaks of light,
Its fruit falling—almost deathless
From an almost heavenly height.

Dew-drunk, the earth receives them
And the shadows pass them over
—As shadows fled from Bethlehem
These shadows flee the clover.

The light lengthens across the earth;
The pinewood is full of life;
What had died has given birth:
The pinewood has found a wife.

WE ARE ALMOST

We are almost near to where the winds blow,
Where to lust is hard and to love easy,
By the gate of the garden where fates grow,
And look up—the watchtower is empty!
But I wonder whether or not the gate
Will open—given it's so very late:
Whether if we knocked, we would be answered,
Whether what we have to say would be heard.
Yes, will it have been worth it? worth our while?
Certainly, I can say—I've been assured.

Do you remember how our star would glow
When we had lost our way in the valley?
That middle blue-black light that used to show,
Yes, I remember it—thought not clearly:
Metal wrecks of mountains, gloomy and great,
Seemed to float in it in spite of their weight;
Yes, we'd seen, or seemed to see, a bluebird,
For a moment, pay reverence—fly backward.
But that was far aback, many a mile.

And I don't know where we or the winds go:
Whether they go to where they do to flee
Or whether there is a home I don't know
Near or on the other side of the sea.
Yes, you and I are, as we were, wayward.
But don't be upset: it's not so absurd
That we two should make our way in this style:
Though we have lost our breath and have blundered.

Look, the garden is near; the sun is low;
There are the scents of flowers, of a tree
On the wind, whispering of faith and woe.
And though it's very late now—can you see
Our father? Once I saw him by the gate
With wild hair, and strange quiet: nothing stirred.
But then he looked at me and gave a word
Lovely to a child in exile.

'Heaped up stones that stand, noising seas that flow,
A honey-laden hive, a busy bee,
Sun-basking clouds, silvery banks of snow:
Yes, there's all that, and there is you and me.'
We will wander all the hour and will wait.

A WILLOW BRANCH

A willow branch, leafless,
In a blue-brown sky
Does not wave, and nonetheless
It seems like a goodbye.

Soon will come the moment
When the sky, stretching, dims,
Takes the tinge of judgement,
And frames frozen limbs.

But do rest assured,
Green will come again;
The willow will have endured
With kinglets in the glen.

And now it is raining.
Feel the little drips.
The purple light is waning
On our immobile lips.

A FRUIT TREE

A fruit tree flowering on a lofty crag
Let its petals fall on a man climbing:
Bronze petals that would flash in the breeze
As the man rushed from jag to jag.
He relished it all—the height, the air, the strange chiming,
And at last came toward the great tree on his knees.

Looking up, he saw the fruits,
Each like a fiery god.
And then he noticed the roots.

CROWDS THAT MEET

Crowds that meet in the city square,
Waves that beat in the sea,
Clouds, even, that greet in the air,
These things—they are free.

But the man alone, standing where the hour is gone,
Whom the world's wide union has forgot:
In his expression there is caught
The look of dawn.

A SEAMSTRESS

A seamstress at peace with the world
Sits and sews and smiles
Like dusk smiles
When the last lights are furled.

The robe she makes is seamless,
Of a sturdy thread,
And
The sleeping world is dreamless,
Lying bare in bed.

But she pricks her finger.

A BIRD OF PREY

A bird of prey in morning light
Gliding desolate lengths
Of grey-blue middle-sky
With great wings upright
And wind-borne strengths
Glinting from its sunward eye
Stretches its body against the sun,
Forcing its pointed face into shadow,
Its gaze turned below
To what is to be won,

And there the changeable sweep
Of earth in its magnitudes
Juts from the black
Reaches of the unfathoming deep
In all its varying attitudes,
Like an amnesiac.

PAN IS IN THE WOOD

Pan is in the wood
And she heard him,
Though he is dead.

There's evil, good
And something grim
Life leaves unsaid
In the dead god's hymn.

MY DAUGHTER

'My daughter, my only daughter,
What a strange crown you wear
Here on this lonesome riverbank
In the cold morning air.
The sky is white, the field is gray,
And the wild tree is bare.'

'I see a ring tied in your locks
Of strange ore and strange make.
I fear it will never come loose
Nor bend nor melt nor break.
And your hands, they seem damp and pale,
And now they seem to shake.'

My father, my only father,
By waters where fates float,
I was alone bathing and saw
A boy in a black boat:
His eyes were white, his face was gray,
And a noose wrung his throat.

With a trembling and outstretched hand,
All wet and all unclad,
I gave to this boy a lily,
For it was all I had,
And he gave me a simple song,
Long and loving and sad.

I climbed up into his black boat
And we sailed through the night,
And for many an hour we gave
New names to every light
That holds up the shivering veil
That hangs at heaven's height.

And then he made for me a crown
More fine than words can tell,
Fit for a love, fit for a queen,
And made of pearl and shell.
He placed it upon me and said,
'Together shall we dwell.'

After the hours had come and gone,
The boat and wind aligned,
And we came upon his palace
And there we danced and dined
And then he gave me this strange ring
To adorn and to bind.

And while he held me in his arms
I saw past him standing
Thousands and thousands of pale girls
Each with a crown and ring,
And cold eyes as white as the sky,
But mouths that could not sing.

With pale hands, they would beckon me
As the moon does the tide.
My father, my only father,
I wept, I shook, I cried,
But my boy led me by the hand
And I became his bride.

Now whenever the tide comes in,
I shall this strange crown wear,
Beyond this lonesome riverbank
And the cold morning air,
As long as this, our sky, is white
And the wild tree is bare.

ON THE BRIDGE

On the bridge between here and there
Is an out-of-place little man
With a tambourine,
Shaking it to his delight.

And why not? The weather is fair
And the prodigious span
Of the bridge would be too serene
Were he elsewhere this night.

A WHISPER

A whisper makes its way
Into the greenery,
Going where it may
Through the scenery.

But it stops at a broken bowl,
Perhaps cast aside during a picnic,
With gilding at the rim.

A PURPLE

A purple abandoned in the dust
Of an impressionist painting;
A music fit for fame and fainting;
Wrought iron meant to rust.

What—in the tones ascending,
The colors caught and blending;
What—the metal mired in time:
Poems all—with a pall of rhyme.

The hues fade; the roar dies;
Genius glimmers to the grave;
Beauty itself closes its eyes
And sleeps a winter in its cave.

EPILOGUE

There went the wind; there went the wild;
There went some songs quite neatly styled;

The dirt is trod; the stones are piled;
The storm has passed; the sky is mild.

Hear of this from a mouth that smiled;
Hear this from the mouth of a child.

Michael Shindler is a writer living in Washington, D.C and a Contributing Editor at *The Vital Center*. His work—which includes essays, poetry, short stories, autobiography, and criticism—has been published in outlets including *Church Life, HillRag, University Bookman, Washington Examiner, Mere Orthodoxy, American Spectator, Providence, Apocalypse Confidential,* and *The North American Anglican*. Since 2019, he has also been a regulator translator of German and Italian prewar poetry, particularly that of Gabriele D'Annunzio.

Milton Keynes UK
Ingram Content Group UK Ltd.
UKHW041946091024
449514UK00006B/52